RAND McNALLY

Mountains

A ***Where Are We?*** Book

by Chris Arvetis
and Carole Palmer
illustrated by James Buckley

Rand McNally for Kids™
Books•Maps•Atlases

Printed in Italy

It certainly is beautiful here.
Look at the hills.
They are really big.

The word *mountain* means a part of the earth's surface rising above the land around it. Mountains have long steep slopes, or sides, narrow or pointed tops (ridges or peaks), and canyons and valleys.

1 Peak
2 Slope
3 Ridge
4 Canyon
5 Valley

Mountains are one of the major landforms on the earth's surface. One-fifth of the land is mountains. Parícutin in Mexico and Vesuvius in Italy are examples of single mountains that tower above the rest of the land.

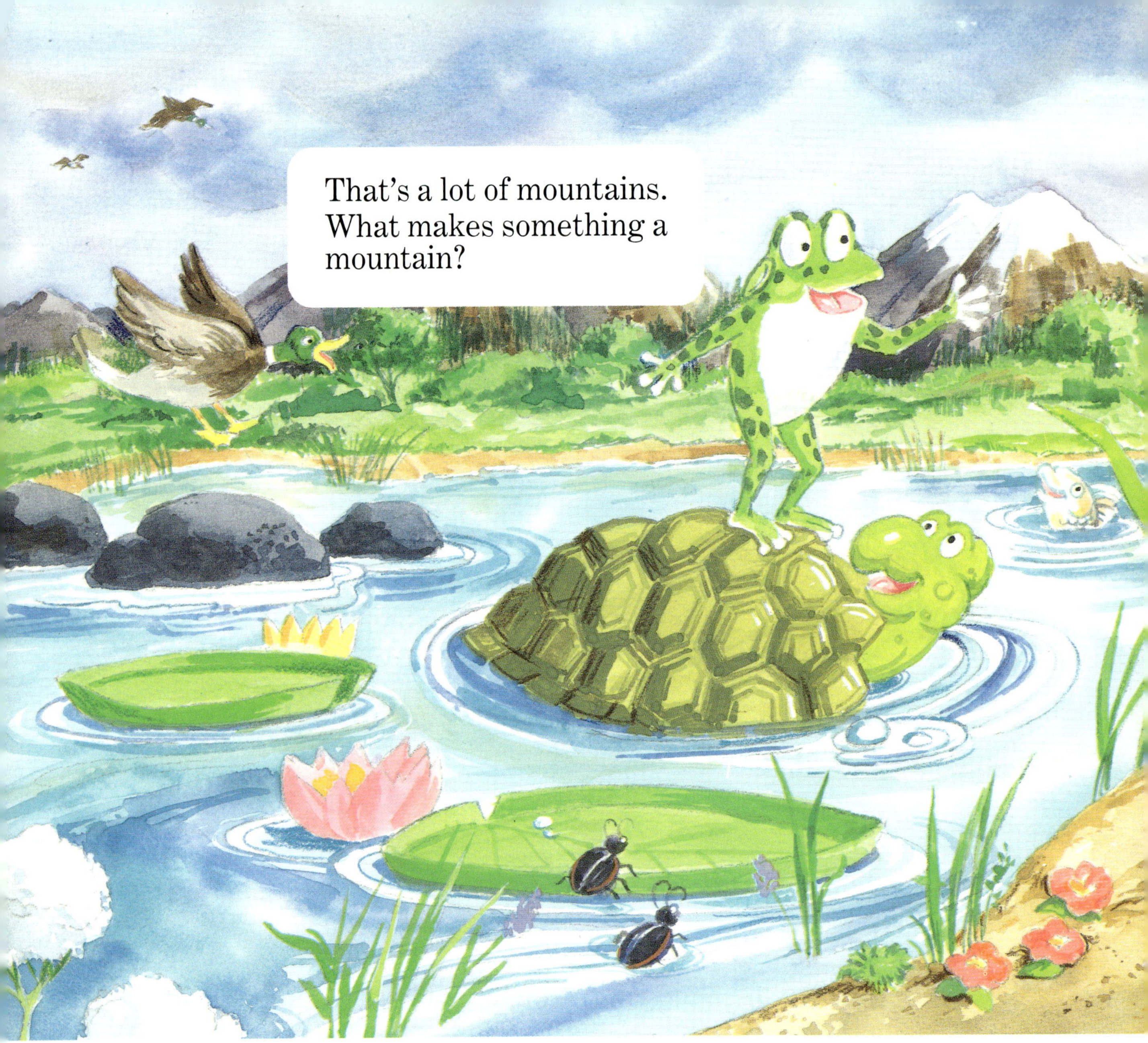

That's a lot of mountains. What makes something a mountain?

Mountains are usually part of a group, or chain, of mountains called a *mountain range.* A group of ranges can form a *mountain system* such as the Rockies, Alps, Andes, and Himalayas. Mountain systems can be part of a larger group called a *mountain belt*.

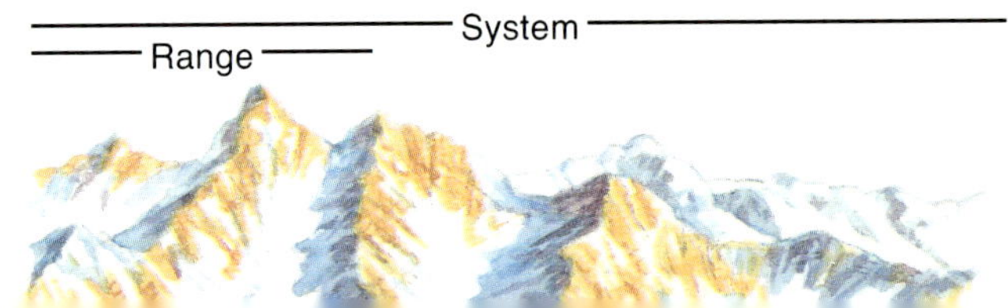

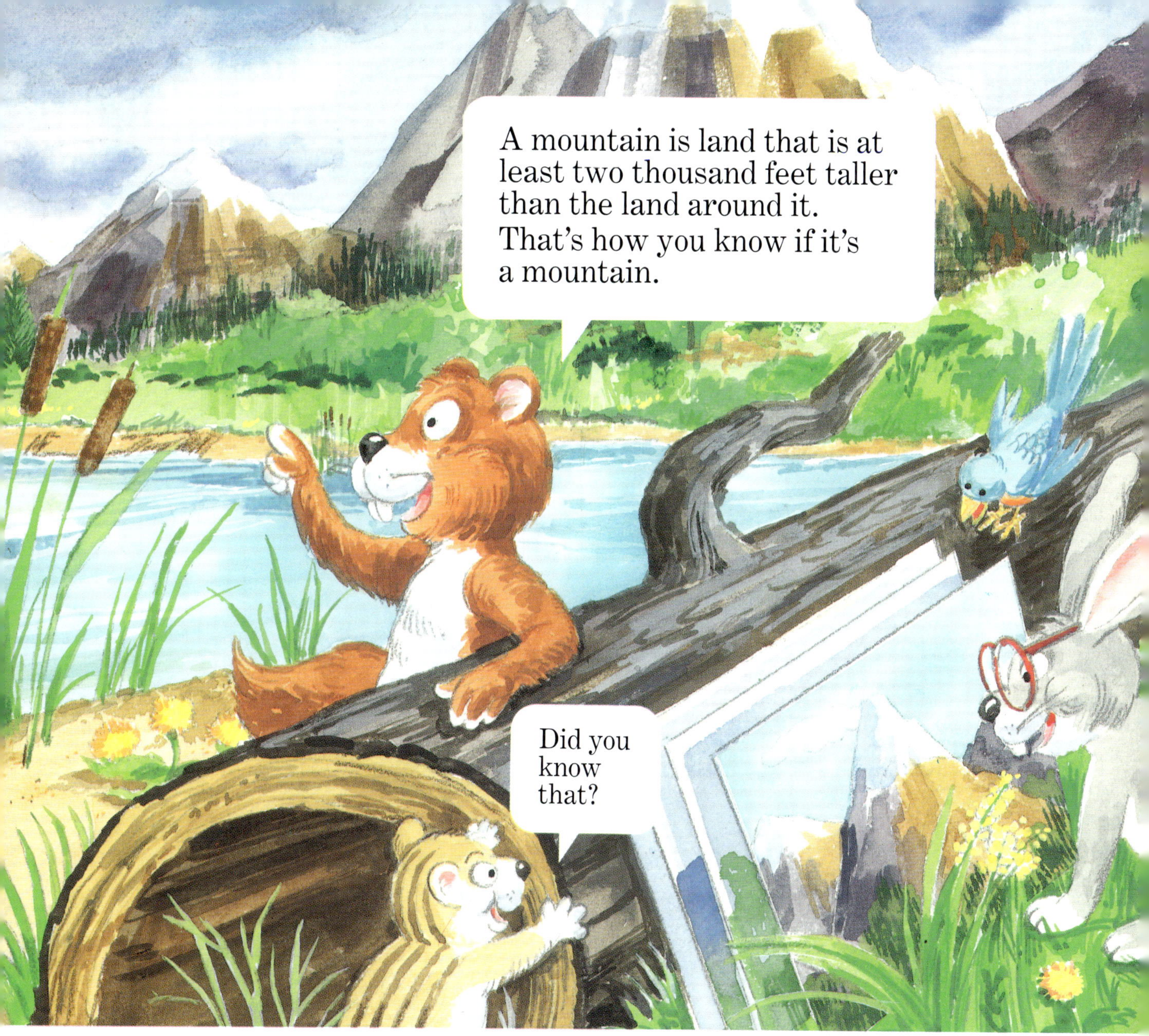

A mountain is land that is at least two thousand feet taller than the land around it. That's how you know if it's a mountain.

Did you know that?

Mountains are also found underwater in the Atlantic, Pacific, and Indian Oceans. These underwater mountains form belts, systems, ranges, and seamounts. Some rise above the surface of the ocean to form islands.

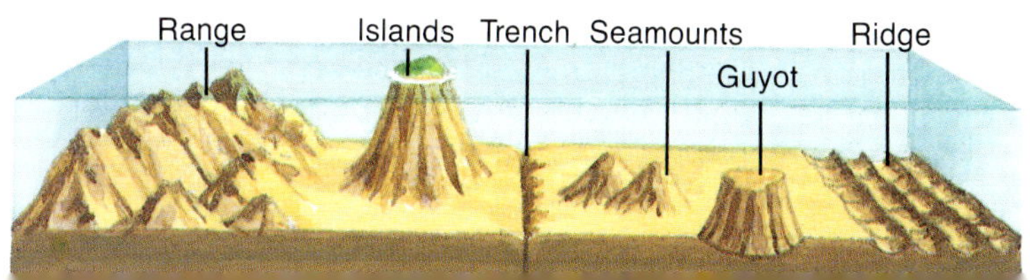

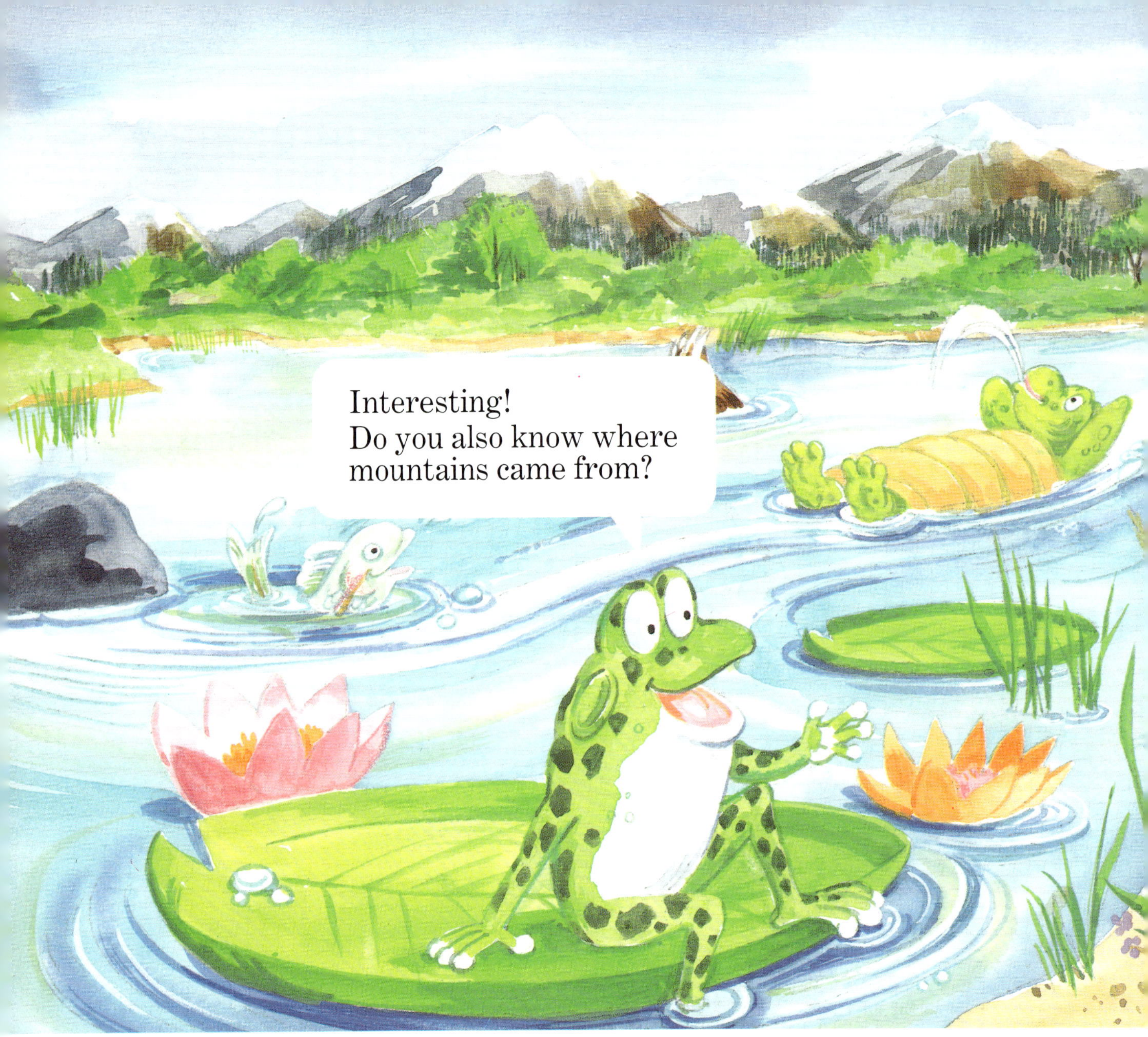

Interesting!
Do you also know where mountains came from?

The earth's outer surface is called its *crust*. This crust is broken into large and small sections called *plates.* The plates moved and caused changes on the earth that formed four basic types of mountains.

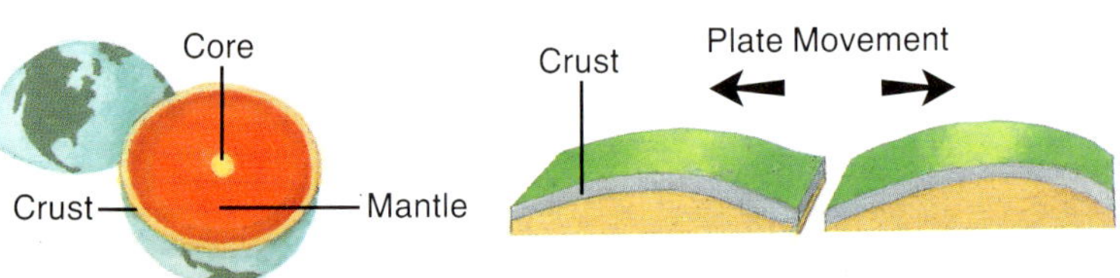

Sure!
Millions of years ago changes within the earth formed them.
Let me show you.
One type of mountain was formed as volcanoes erupted.
The layers of lava piled up until they made a mountain.

The red stuff is lava.

Mount Fuji in Japan and Mount Rainier in Washington are well-known *volcanic mountains.* The Hawaiian Islands are made up of 132 islands created by a line of volcanoes.

Hawaiian Islands

Another type of mountain is a dome mountain. This type of mountain was formed as the earth's surface was forced up, creating a dome shape.

Wind and water wear down, or *erode*, mountains. Over time, *dome mountains* are carved into peaks and valleys. The Black Hills of South Dakota and the Adirondacks of New York are dome mountains.

Many of the mountains were formed when layers of rock in the earth's crust were pushed together and folded.
Look at these layers of rock.
As the rocks wrinkled, the layers formed folded mountains.

I see the wrinkles.

Many of the world's mountains are *folded mountains.* The Appalachians in the United States have gently folded rock layers while the Alps of Europe were folded with such force that the layers turned upside down.

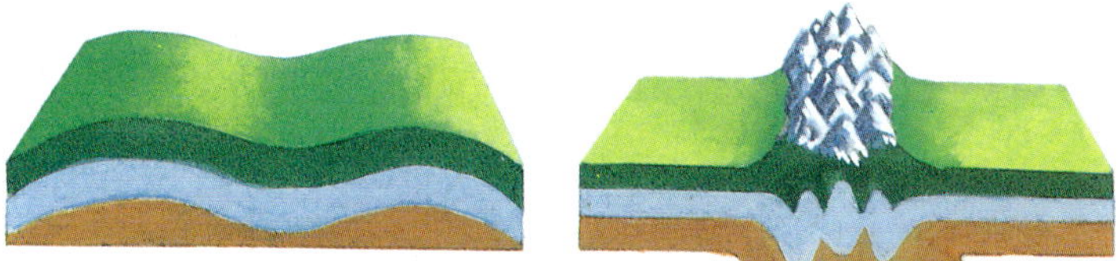

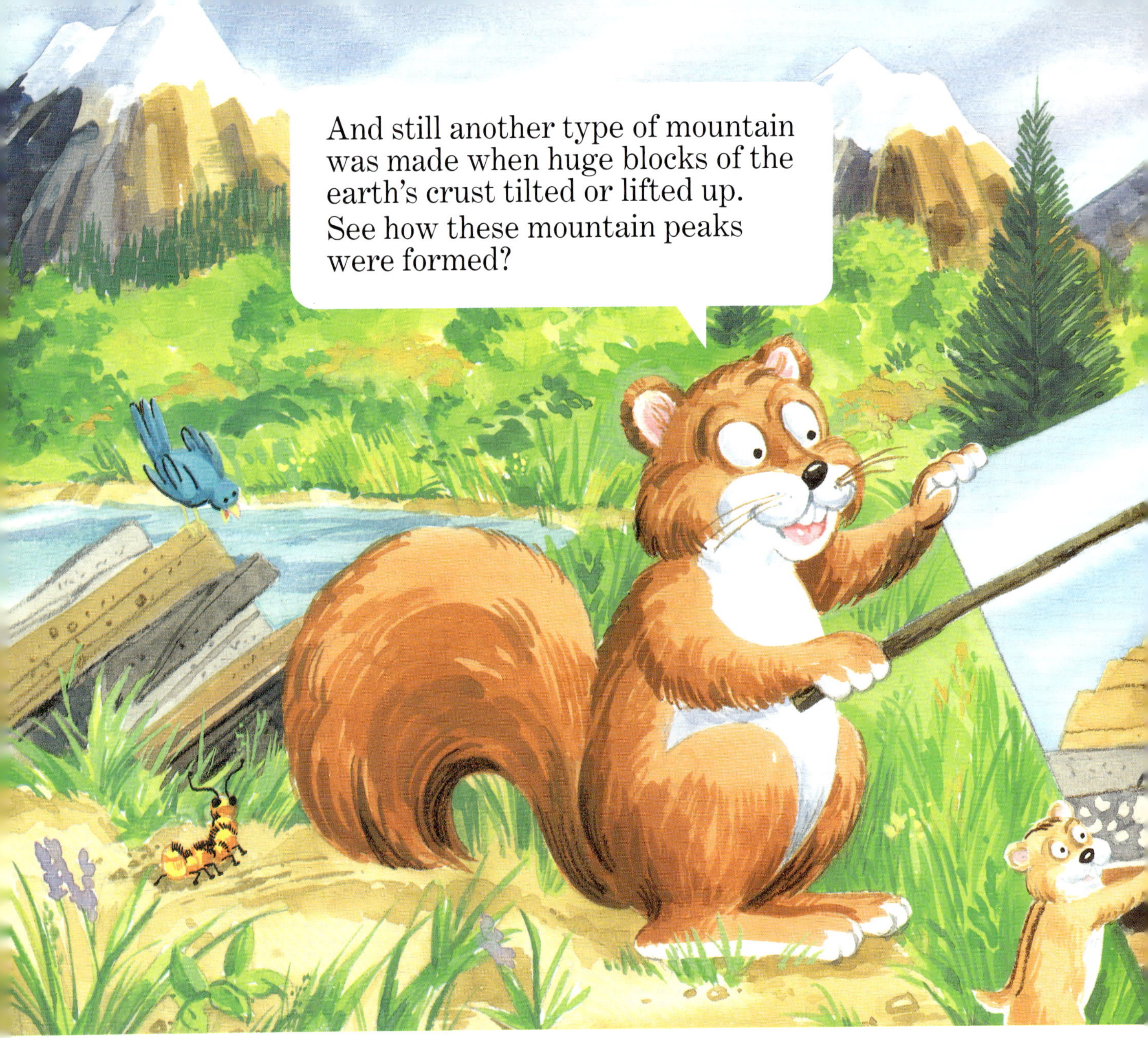

And still another type of mountain was made when huge blocks of the earth's crust tilted or lifted up. See how these mountain peaks were formed?

Fault-block mountains are formed along a crack called a *fault*. The San Andreas fault in California runs for nearly 620 miles. Earthquakes are common in areas near faults.

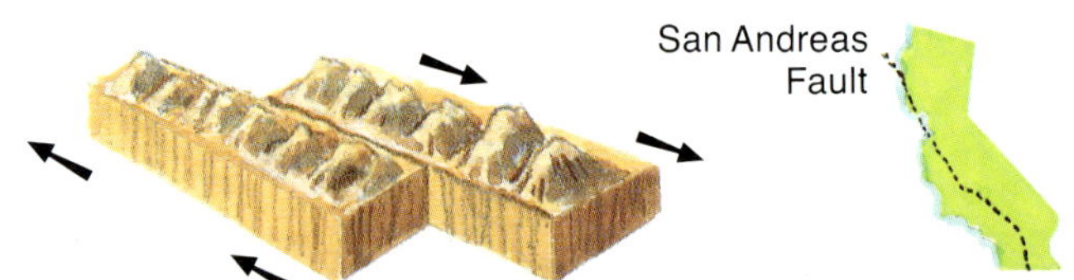

Interesting!

The Harz Mountains in Germany, the Tien Shan in central Asia, and the Atlas in Northern Africa are fault-block mountains. Many mountain systems of the world were formed by a combination of mountain-making ways.

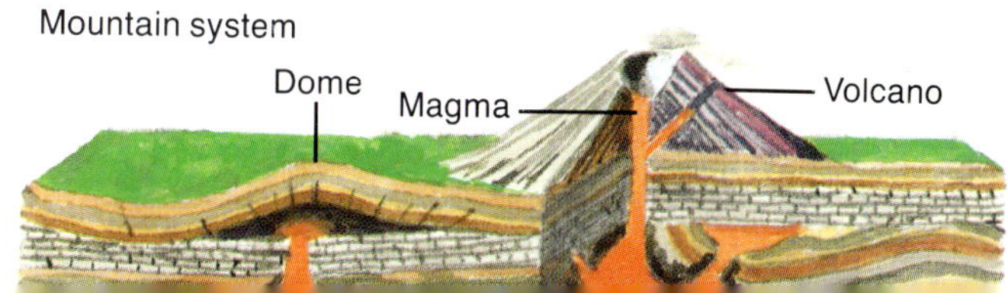

But let's go!
We are going to find out more about the mountains.
Here in the valley, trees and grass grow, and cattle and sheep graze in the summer.

A *valley* is the lowland between hills or mountains. The sides of a valley are its walls or slopes, and the bottom is the valley floor. This mountain valley is used as pastureland.

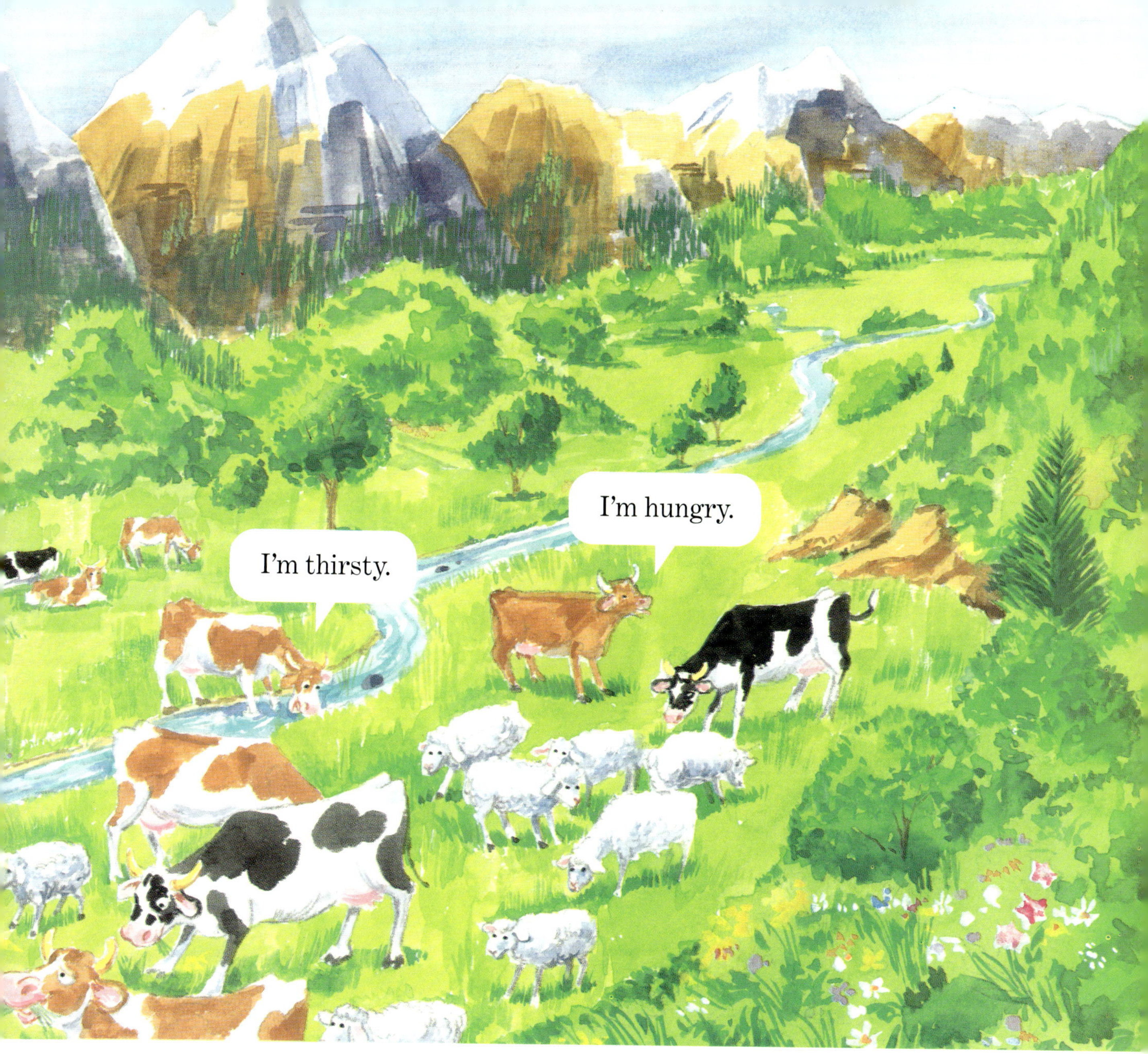

I'm thirsty.

I'm hungry.

The mountain peaks are high above the valley floor. The height, or *elevation,* of a mountain is given as its distance above sea level. Mount Everest is the world's highest mountain at 29,028 feet.

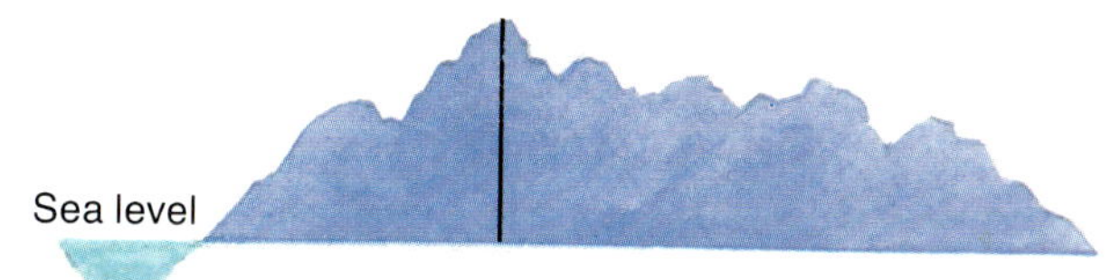

It's cold.

Brrr.

Many kinds of trees can be found in the mountain forests. There are the giant redwoods, firs, cedars, and spruces in the western coastal ranges of the United States. Beech, birch, maple, elm, and white pine can be found in the northeastern United States.

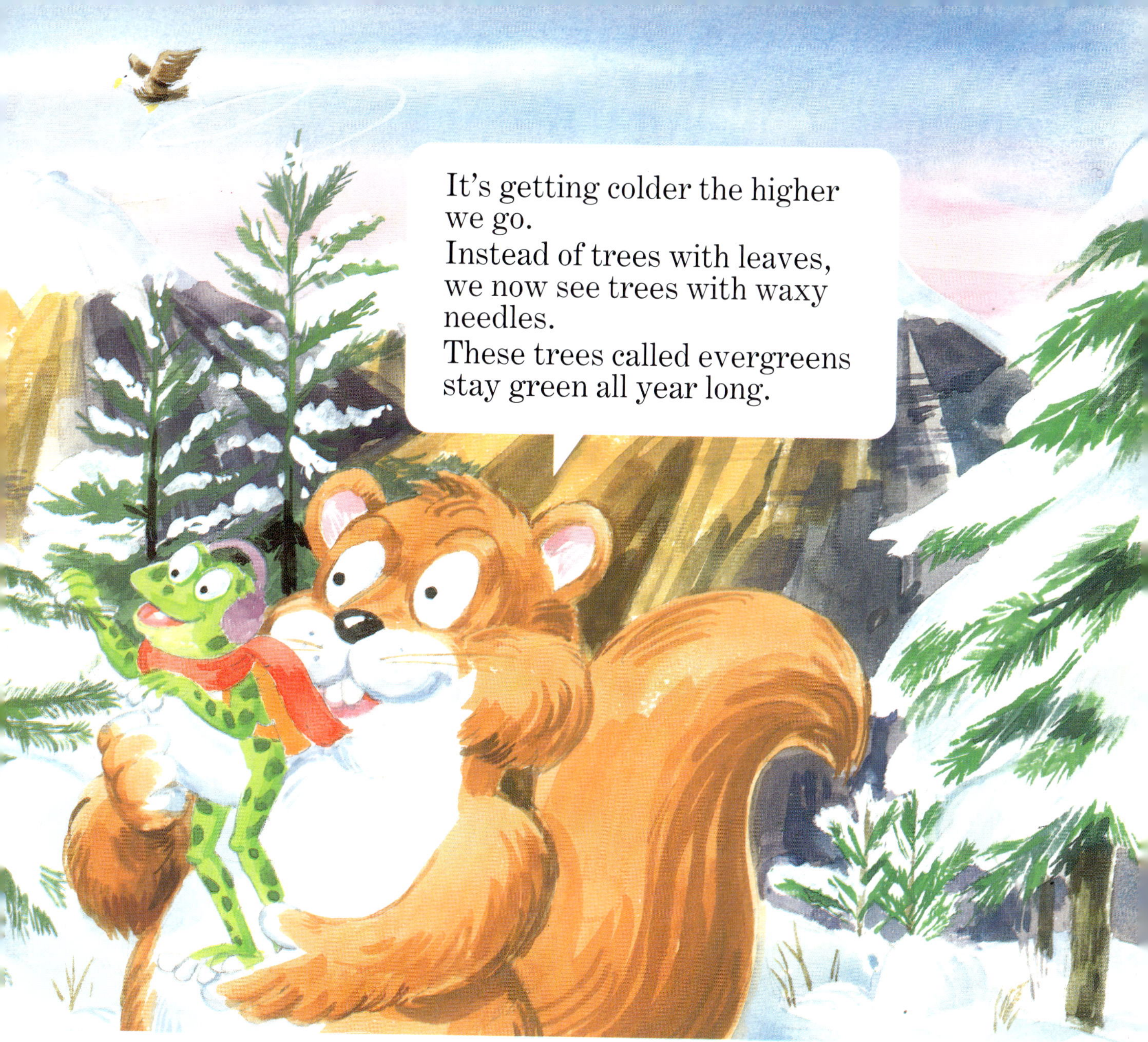

It's getting colder the higher we go.
Instead of trees with leaves, we now see trees with waxy needles.
These trees called evergreens stay green all year long.

In tropical mountain areas, hardwood trees such as mahogany, teak, rosewood, and ebony grow. The lumber industry uses many of the trees from mountain areas for wood products.

The trees block out the sunlight, so we see ferns and mosses growing on the ground in the shade. Chickadees, woodpeckers, and warblers live here. Owls, hawks, and eagles can also be found.

1 Woodpecker
2 Warbler
3 Hawk
4 Chickadee
5 Eagle

In the high mountain areas, wild flowers such as the alpine forget-me-not, sheep laurel, and white phlox can survive the cold winters. In Europe and Asia, edelweiss grows in the high mountains. It has a beautiful star-shaped flower.

Edelweiss

Alpine forget-me-not

5

This moss looks very soft.

It is soft.

4

In warmer climates, crops are grown on terraced mountainsides. Sugar, wheat, barley, cacao, and potatoes are planted in the South American Andes.

Hares and squirrels play in the forest.
Larger animals like deer, elk, and caribou also live in the mountains.

1 Squirrel
2 Hare
3 Caribou
4 Elk
5 Deer

Most living things have to adjust to mountain conditions. Mountain air is thin and has less oxygen than air at sea level. Mountain animals have developed larger hearts and lungs to help them get all the oxygen their bodies need.

Mountain lion
Mountain goat

Hi!

The animals may also have thick coats that protect them from the cold. Some animals, such as the snow leopard, have large paws that act like snowshoes. Other animals have hoofs that grip to help them travel the narrow ledges and sharp ridges.

Snow leopard

Look at the wolves, foxes, lynxes and weasels.
Even black bears and mountain lions roam around.

Some mountain animals are plant eaters. These animals must live at levels where plants can be found. Sheep, goats, and deer are plant eaters. The ibex, bighorn sheep, and wapiti are some common grazing animals.

Bighorn sheep

Ibex

Those bears are always eating.

1 Wolves
2 Fox
3 Lynx
4 Mtn. Lion
5 Bear
6 Weasel

Some mountain animals are meat eaters that hunt and kill other animals for food. Mountain lions, lynxes, wolves, and red foxes are meat eaters. Animals, such as bears, are both plant eaters and meat eaters. They eat fish, small animals, nuts, and berries.

Bear

From here we can see the valley below with the cattle and sheep grazing.
This ridge is a perfect place to view the mountain valley and canyon.

Mountains were formed many millions of years ago. Since that time, the forces of nature have worn away the mountains and changed the land features. Humans have also changed the mountains. They have built roads and tunnels, cut down trees, and created mines and quarries.

The towering mountain peaks are a land feature that attracts mountain climbers. Edmund Hillary of New Zealand and Tenzing Norgay of Nepal were the first climbers to reach the top of Mount Everest on May 29, 1953.

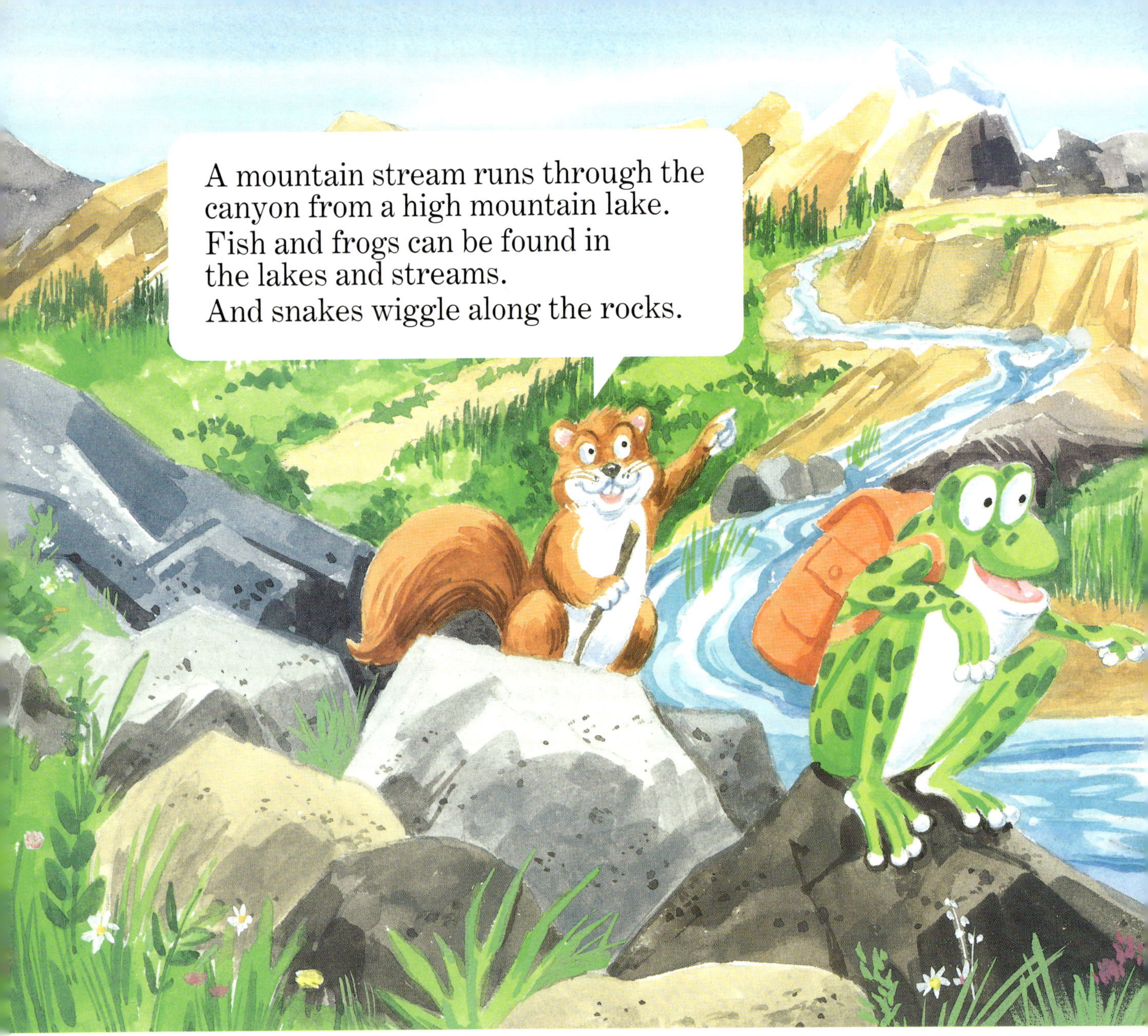

A mountain stream runs through the canyon from a high mountain lake. Fish and frogs can be found in the lakes and streams. And snakes wiggle along the rocks.

High mountain peaks affect the weather by blocking the moving air and causing rain or snow. The rain and snow create the water supply that makes the streams and rivers. The Rio Grande, Ural, and Amazon are rivers that begin in the mountains.

Lakes can also be found in the mountains. Lake Titicaca in the Andes is the world's highest lake. Water from the high lakes and rivers is often used by power plants, which change falling waters into electric power.

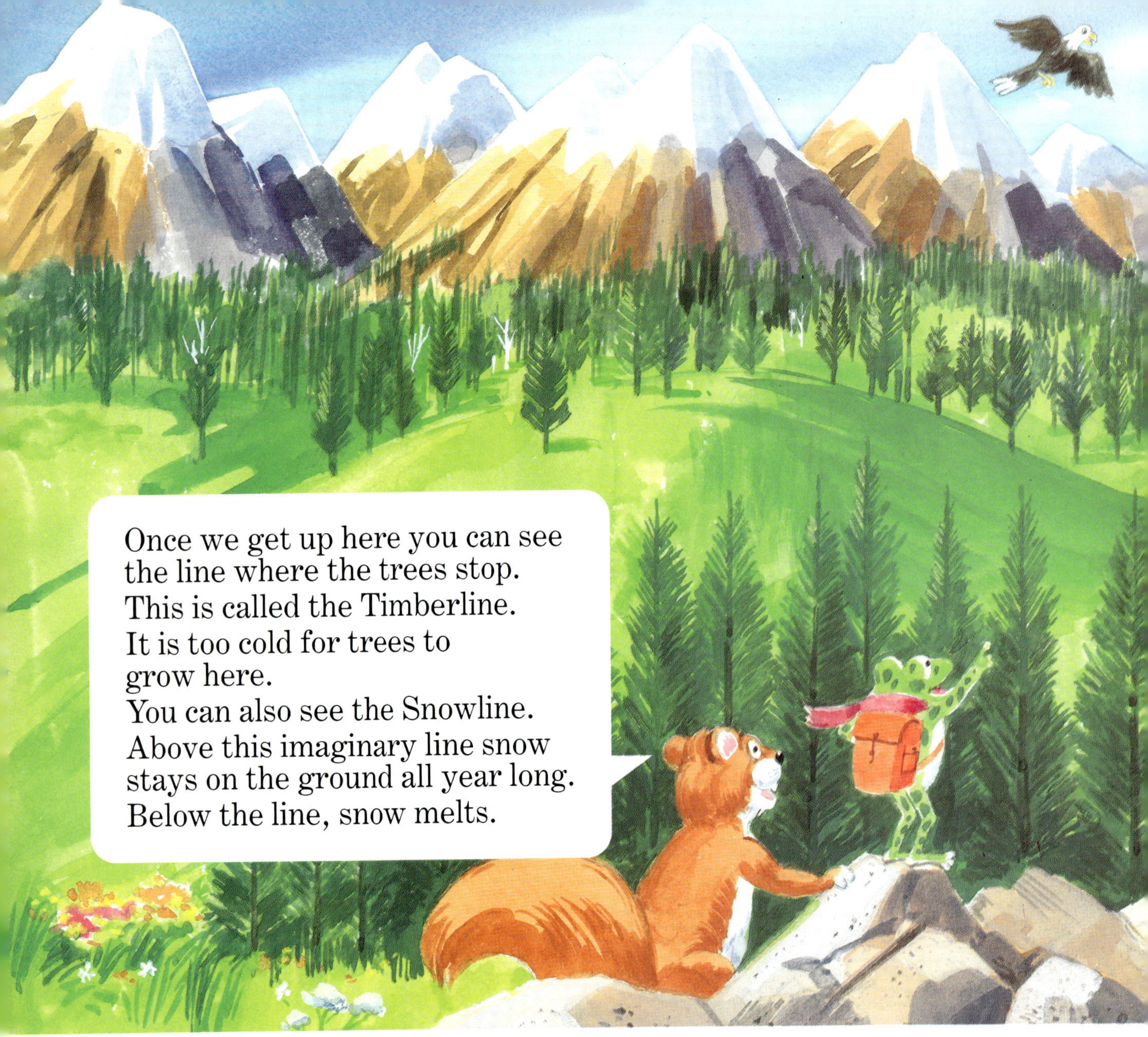

Once we get up here you can see the line where the trees stop. This is called the Timberline. It is too cold for trees to grow here. You can also see the Snowline. Above this imaginary line snow stays on the ground all year long. Below the line, snow melts.

Timberline can be found at different heights. It depends on the climate of the area. In the Canadian Rockies, timberline is at 9,000 to 9,500 feet, while in the Andes of Peru, timberline is usually higher than 13,000 feet.

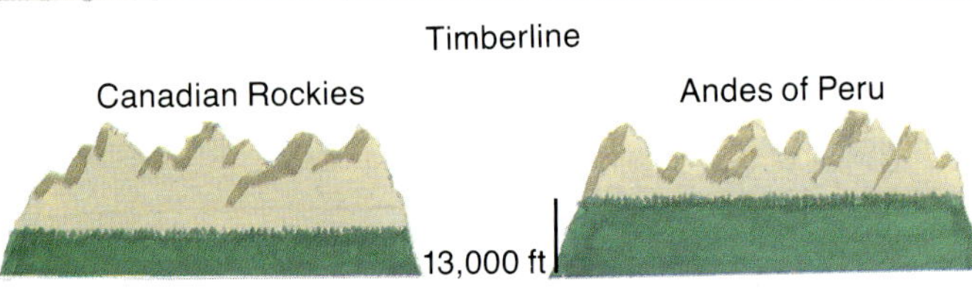

Snowline varies with the amount of snowfall, the amount of sunshine, and mountain height. Snowline in the mountains near the equator is at almost 18,000 feet, while it is just a few feet above sea level in Antarctica, Greenland, and Alaska.

Snowline

Antarctica Snowline

Snowline near Equator

2 ft

18,000 ft

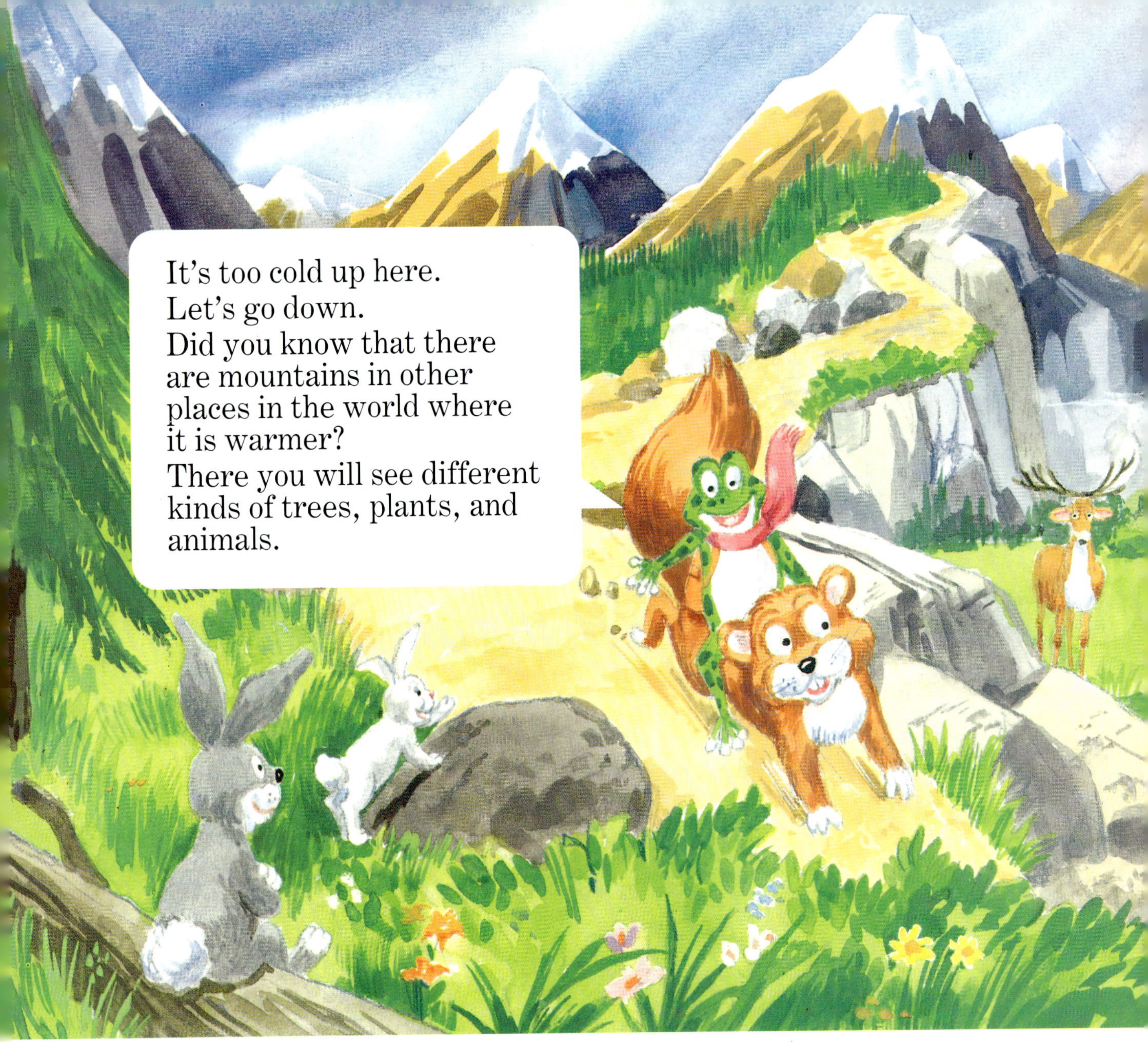

It's too cold up here.
Let's go down.
Did you know that there are mountains in other places in the world where it is warmer?
There you will see different kinds of trees, plants, and animals.

In South America, tropical forests with thick growths of moss-covered trees are part of the mountain areas of Brazil and Venezuela. The llama, vicuña and alpaca are animals found in the tropical forests of the Andes.

In Africa, bamboo grows at lower levels in the mountains. Higher up, cypress pine and cedars grow. The hyrax, forest elephant, leopard, and mountain gorilla roam in the mountains.

Hyrax

Gorilla

The highest mountain peak for each of these seven continents is shown. The elevation for each peak is also listed.

Kilimanjaro
19,340 ft
Africa

Vinson Massif
16,066 ft
Antarctica

Elbrus
18,510 ft
Europe

Yes, I'm tired too!
You'd really be tired if you climbed the highest mountain in the world, Mount Everest, or the tallest mountain in Africa, Kilimanjaro.
Everest 29,028 ft Asia
Kosciusko 7,277 ft Australia
McKinley 20,320 ft North America
Aconcagua 22,834 ft South America

The world's mountain landscape makes a majestic and beautiful sight. Now can you tell me all about mountains?

Time for a nap.

Whether skiing in the Alps in Switzerland or viewing Mauna Loa in Hawaii, people everywhere enjoy the beauty of mountains.